The Seed Of Resurrection

(Discover How To Overcome Sin, Abandonment, Rejection, Hopelessness, Confusion, Shame & Guilt)

By

Anthony Montoya

The Seed Of Resurrection

(Discover How To Overcome Sin, Abandonment, Rejection, Hopelessness, confusion, shame & Guilt)

By

Anthony Montoya

Copyright 2014
All Rights Reserved
Printed in the United States of America

Published By

ABM Publications
A division of Andrew Bills Ministries,, Inc.
PO Box 6811, Orange, CA 92863
www.abmpublications.com

ISBN: 978-1-931820-13-4

All scripture quotations, unless otherwise indicated are taken from the King James Version of the Bible, Public Domain. Those marked AMP are from the Amplified Bible, copyright @ 1987, The Updated Edition, by the Zondervan Corporation and the Lockman Foundation, and is used by permission. All rights reserved.

DEDICATION

To my spiritual parents,
Apostle Santiago & Prophetess Mary Anduljar

And my daughter,
Alexis Marina Montoya

Table Of Contents

	Forward	7
	About The Author	9
	Introduction	13
1	The Seed Of Resurrection	15
2	Misconceptions Revealed	21
3	Sowing	25
4	Tithing	31
5	The Parable Of The Sower	35
6	Different Winds Of Doctrine	45
7	Our Inheritance	55
	Ministry Contact Information	59

Foreward

It is with much excitement and honor that I get the opportunity to acquaint you with my friend Anthony Montoya. In his unique style he reflects authentic leadership, tempered by a deep compassion for the lost. In this age of religious phonies and spiritual apathy, Anthony does not compromise the unfailing word of God.

His passion and exuberance for God is infectious; Challenging Christians to draw closer to God and take the Bible serious. During a time I was seeking a speaker for my Ministry, God said to me "call Anthony". God used Anthony to confirm some important future Ministry events that He had already spoken to me about. For the reasons above, and others that followed, I look forward to future Ministry with Anthony where his gifts will edify and be a blessing to the Body of Christ.

Lilly Avila

Rays of Glory Ministries, Inc.

In all the 19 years that I have known Anthony Montoya, he has been very poised and consistent. He's a man I know who rightly divides the Word of truth. He carefully hears from the Holy Spirit and he speaks as the Spirit gives him the utterance. I highly recommend his work to any reader out there.

Lloyd Nsek

Author of *"Christianity the End of Spiritual Confusion"*

Anthony Montoya

About The Author

Hello family, I'm just going to give you a brief illustration of my testimony about me and my life In Yahshua. I'm currently divorced over 10 years one daughter, my daughter is 13 one of the greatest life's experiences in my life. My parents are Ministers of the good news for the last 45years experience in the prophetic call and commission. My father's an Apostle and my mother's a Prophetess, who's been used for 17 years. I've been trained under the Holy Spirit and will always be in training, ever since my walk I've been taught to die to self and to lay down my own self will for the sake of the Kingdom for transformation. My biological father left me when I was 11, I had an encounter with God himself, the Father when I was 18 years of age.

One day everyone was gone, my mother had three children I am the middle child, it was around midnight walking around my home. I spoke to myself and stated I was all alone then the phone rang it was weird, then I said hello the voice said" Are you alone" I then said who is this. The voice continued and said "This is your Father, your not alone." Then I said, "ok who is this, stop playing around!" The voice continued and said, "Go to the mirror and then stated are you alone?" Then I said, "Who is this the voice?" Then he continued, "This is your Father in Heaven." I was stunned for that moment and couldn't grasp or understand the situation and my brain went blank.

Since that day, I've been divorced ten years, slept in the streets homeless for about 6 years, kicked out of churches for being too prophetic, slept in houses with ministers who are apostles and prophets that astro projected out of their bodies.

While I have disobeyed Yahweh several times, he allowed me to see the demonic realm and was attacked heavily by my own disobedience, also by other leaders that have mastered the gift inside them using for their own self gain. Trained under the gift of the discerning of spirits, to discern the motive and intents of the hearts of the people around me.

I was just recently pulled out from being homeless, several years ago about 2 ½ to be precise, generational curses broken off from biological father who made a deal with Satan, An apostle prophesied and stated your biological father made a deal with Satan to have the blood of two of his children for promise for money for the rest of his life. My sister was cured from whooping cough there was no cure at that time. I was set free from several demonic spirits that are so real. My walk in ministry was to discern why so much division, only by Yahshua's grace and the Holy Spirit has graced me to understand the spirit of influence & religion using venom of false doctrine and false prophecies that's been impregnated in the hearts of gods children & have been left crippled and shuts down their own immune system.

My present state I'm ordained minister, my belief is to be a life living sacrifice for Yahweh's kingdom , only to be servant to others and help one another reach Yahweh's purpose n destiny in our lives. To unveil the mysteries and revelations of this kingdom age for all his children to be set free from religion, jezebel spirits, spirit of influence, psychology, false hope (false prophesies), rejection, abandonment guilt, shame, control, seared conscious, subconscious, conscious, mesmoratic cells, trauma, familiar spirits, camellia spirits that transforms and changes color, cockatrice spirit, the false god of Prosperity, Fortune & Destiny, mystical influences that general spirits have had dominion over us.

Isaiah 26: 13-14 (AMP) says, "O Lord, our God, other masters besides You have ruled over us, but we will acknowledge *and* mention Your name only.[14] They [the former tyrant masters] are dead, they shall not live *and* reappear; they are powerless ghosts, they shall not rise *and* come back. Therefore You have visited and made an end of them and caused every memory of them [every trace of their supremacy] to perish." This reference speaks of general demonic spirits even with all religious practices, he will even wipe away the memory of them out of us.

Anthony Montoya

Anthony Montoya

Introduction

Family, what you are about to read has wandered through Christian beliefs and doctrines. It states in the word to be careful and refrain from myths, fables and endless genealogies and speculation of people's talk rather than stewardship and trust in Yahweh's redemptive plan of love and belief.

You can assure yourself to be free from guilt, shame, unworthiness, false hope, rejection and abandonment. It gives precise specific understanding where it's derived from.

Family, we all as a whole need to be very careful and refrain from the spirit of religion and influence. We must come to the end of self, die to self and lay down our own self will.

In most cases, human beings live off of our own self=centeredness and what has been falsely impregnatedd in our spirits, eggs that were thrown by teachings, prophecies and impartations using reverse parapsychology influences. You may be wondering how, someone who has a big title, great name, the ministry involved in your circle or friendship, using the gifts and talents in the name of God. Selling the birth and death of his resurrection, we need to ask the Holy Spirit to show us the motive and intentions of the heart of others and to ask for the discernment of discerning of spirits which the body lacks greatly.

Anthony Montoya

Chapter One

The Seed Of Resurrection

Many people have wandered through carnal and spiritual indecisiveness with their conscious struggling with their subconscious as the battlefield is being played out in their mind. These struggles usually cause tension or warfare within as many seek to be led by the Holy Spirit.

Deep concerns have ravaged through the minds of man and his predecessors as he seeks to follow the commands or directives of Yahweh and understand the full meaning of biblical principles.

Hebrews 4:12 (AMP) says, **"For the Word that Yahweh speaks is alive and full of power (making it active, operative, energizing and effective); it is sharper than any two-edged sword, penetrating to the dividing line of the breath of life (soul) and (the immortal) spirit, and of joints and marrow (of the deepest parts of our nature), exposing and sifting and analyzing and judging the very thoughts and purposes of the heart."**

Let's analyze such perdition able matters of anarchy in response to Romans 6:5 (AMP) which says, **"For if we have become one with Him by sharing a death like His, we shall also be (one with Him in sharing) His resurrection (by a new life lived for Yahweh).**

Now an illustration combining these two injunctions intervening for its attentive substances referring to Job 1: 6-7 (AMP) which says, **"Now there was a day when the sons (the angels) of Yahweh came to present themselves** before the king, and Satan (the adversary and accuser) also came among them, And the king said to Satan, From where did you come? Then Satan answered the Lord, from going to and fro on the earth and from walking up and down on it."

As we focus particularly on these verses, we're dealing with highly intellectually state of intelligence, methodical, philosophical, religious and psychological warfare accumulating in the Body of Christ (Yahshua) his church (House, Kingdom).

Coming to this point of conclusion, its paralytic assertions, notice only Yahshua himself could identify who this Angel of light or spirit was sitting there amongst the family and no one else, meaning the bible speaks of in every congregation or group only one percentage of you all can identify the gift of Discerning of spirits, which the body lacks greatly.

The reader may question and ask, "What are you trying to say or am I saying?" It is what it is, the heavenly Father created the gifts and talents of the natural and spiritual side.

The reader also may be asking, "How can we identify spiritual confusion?" It's possible you cannot, the reader needs more dying, breaking of death to self, endlessly in need of spiritual training in order to perceive false hope, hope differed, receiving seeds within your heart, mind, body, soul, spirit, emotions and feelings, etc. Paralytic dogmatic formalities to drive you to act against your own will or indecisiveness, to fleece and strip you of all things trapping you to leave you abandoned without understanding left astray and spiritually crippled!

In terms, let's analyze 1 Corinthians 12: 1-11 (AMP) which says, "**Now about the spiritual gifts (the special endowments of supernatural energy), brethren, I do not want you to be misinformed.**

² You know that when you were heathen, you were led off after idols that could not speak [habitually] as impulse directed *and* **whenever the occasion might arise.**

³ Therefore I want you to understand that no one speaking under the power *and* **influence of the [Holy] Spirit of God can [ever] say, Jesus be cursed! And no one can [really] say, Jesus is [my] Lord, except by** *and* **under the power** *and* **influence of the Holy Spirit.**

⁴ Now there are distinctive varieties *and* **distributions of endowments (gifts, [a]extraordinary powers distinguishing certain Christians, due to the power of divine grace operating in their souls by the Holy Spirit) and they vary, but the [Holy] Spirit remains the same.**

⁵ And there are distinctive varieties of service *and* **ministration, but it is the same Lord [Who is served].**

⁶ And there are distinctive varieties of operation [of working to accomplish things], but it is the same God Who inspires *and* **energizes them all in all.**

⁷ But to each one is given the manifestation of the [Holy] Spirit [the evidence, the spiritual illumination of the Spirit] for good *and* **profit.**

⁸ To one is given in *and* **through the [Holy] Spirit [the power to speak] a message of wisdom, and to another**

[the power to express] a word of knowledge *and* understanding according to the same [Holy] Spirit;

⁹ To another [[b]wonder-working] faith by the same [Holy] Spirit, to another the extraordinary powers of healing by the one Spirit;

¹⁰ To another the working of miracles, to another prophetic insight ([c]the gift of interpreting the divine will and purpose); to another the ability to discern *and* distinguish between [the utterances of true] spirits [and false ones], to another various kinds of [unknown] tongues, to another the ability to interpret [such] tongues.

¹¹ All these [gifts, achievements, abilities] are inspired *and* brought to pass by one and the same [Holy] Spirit, Who apportions to each person individually [exactly] as He chooses.

Then in Acts 16:16-21 (AMP) it says, **"As we were on our way to the place of prayer, we were met by a slave girl who was possessed by a spirit of divination [claiming to foretell future events and to discover hidden knowledge], and she brought her owners much gain by her fortunetelling.**

¹⁷ She kept following Paul and [the rest of] us, shouting loudly, These men are the servants of the Most High God! They announce to you the way of salvation!

¹⁸ And she did this for many days. Then Paul, being sorely annoyed *and* worn out, turned and said to the spirit

within her, I charge you in the name of Jesus Christ to come out of her! And it came out that very [a]moment.

[19] But when her owners discovered that their hope of profit was gone, they caught hold of Paul and Silas and dragged them before the authorities in the forum (marketplace), [where trials are held].

[20] And when they had brought them before the magistrates, they declared, These fellows are Jews and they are throwing our city into great confusion.

[21] They encourage the practice of customs which it is unlawful for us Romans to accept or observe!"

There are several conclusions familiar spirits drive you to interpret falsely on your own accord, which brings favor and prosperity if you can identify with it and make covenant with it. You can actually receive favorable prosperity from false gods, because the angel of light and the host of the second heavens (mystery revelation) territorial and ancestral brings false hope, hope differed being impregnated and birthed falsely and leads you astray to become so ignorant of Satan's devices.

Again, notice verse 19' **"But when her owners discovered that their hope of profit was gone, they caught hold of Paul and Silas and dragged them before the authorities in the forum (marketplace), [where trials are held]."**

Let's read 1 Corinthians 10: 20-21 (AMP), **"No, I am suggesting that what the pagans sacrifice they offer [in effect] to demons (to evil spiritual powers) and not to**

God [at all]. I do not want you to fellowship *and* be partners with diabolical spirits [by eating at their feasts].

[21] You cannot drink the Lord's cup and the demons' cup. You cannot partake of the Lord's table and the demons' table."

Chapter Two

Misconceptions Revealed

To become indignant against your own fallacy (in logic and rhetoric, a fallacy is incorrect reasoning in argumentation resulting in a misconception).

Proverb 21:22 (AMP) says, **"A wise man scales the city walls of the mighty and brings down the stronghold in which they trust."**

Now, let's back track a few verses back to verse 16, which says, **"A man who wanders out of the way of understanding shall abide in the congregation of the spirits (of the dead)."** Receive the baptism of the Holy Spirit and Fire now in Yahshua's name.

Permit me to indulge deeper and let's read 2 Chronicles 33: 1-6 (AMP), **"Manasseh was twelve years old when he began to reign, and he reigned fifty-five years in Jerusalem.**

² But he did evil in the Lord's sight, like the abominations of the heathen whom the Lord drove out before the Israelites.

³ For he built again the [idolatrous] high places which Hezekiah his father had broken down, and he reared altars for the Baals and made the Asherim and worshiped all the hosts of the heavens and served them.

⁴ Also he built [heathen] altars in the Lord's house, of which the Lord had said, In Jerusalem shall My Name be forever.

⁵ He built altars for all the hosts of the heavens in the two courts of the Lord's house.

⁶ And he burned his children as an offering [to his god] in the Valley of Ben-hinnom [son of Hinnom], and practiced soothsaying, augury, and sorcery, and dealt with mediums and wizards. He did much evil in the sight of the Lord, provoking Him to anger.

Here is another assertion of how do you know what spirit is being operated or controlled by just because the congregation holds many people many followers of few followers,, religion perceives that if you have followers it's called fruit wrong!

Many shall come and say that I am the Christ meaning, the gift, the calling, the positions (title, followers etc.) and the anointing of God is irrevocable without repentance, manifesting and presumptuously moving without the presence of God. Acting like it talking like it and even demonstrating it through the gift but the motive and intent of the heart is wicked and lost. Even using it in the name of Jesus Christ.

Deuteronomy 10: 16-19 (AMP) says, **"So circumcise the foreskin of your [minds and] hearts; be no longer stubborn *and* hardened.** Christians are you being circumcised, dying to self, asking for self-revelation to see yourself or your being driven to sow seeds of money and tithing (oops we will get to that in a bit) like you can buy God's favor, anointing and grace?

Ephesians 4: 17-19 (AMP) says, "**So this I say and solemnly testify in [the name of] the Lord [as in His presence], that you must no longer live as the heathen (the Gentiles) do in their perverseness [in the folly, vanity, and emptiness of their souls and the futility] of their minds.**

18 Their [a]moral understanding is darkened *and* their reasoning is beclouded. [They are] alienated (estranged, self-banished) from the life of God [with no share in it; this is] because of the ignorance (the want of knowledge and perception, the willful blindness) that is [b]deep-seated in them, due to their hardness of heart [to the insensitiveness of their moral nature].

19 In their spiritual apathy they have become callous *and* past feeling *and* reckless and have abandoned themselves [a prey] to unbridled sensuality, eager *and* greedy to indulge in every form of impurity [that their depraved desires may suggest and demand].

Ephesians 4:7 (AMP) says, "**Yet grace (God's unmerited favor) was given to each of us individually (not indiscriminately, but in different ways) in proportion to the measure of Christ's (rich and bounteous) gift.**

Ephesians 5:7-11 (AMP) says, "**So do not associate *or* be sharers with them.**

8 For once you were darkness, but now you are light in the Lord; walk as children of Light [lead the lives of those native-born to the Light].

⁹ For the fruit (the effect, the product) of the Light *or* [a]*the Spirit* [consists] in every form of kindly goodness, uprightness of heart, and trueness of life.

¹⁰ And try to learn [in your experience] what is pleasing to the Lord [let your lives be constant proofs of what is most acceptable to Him].

¹¹ Take no part in *and* have no fellowship with the fruitless deeds *and* enterprises of darkness, but instead [let your lives be so in contrast as to] [b]expose *and* reprove *and* convict them.

Chapter Three

Sowing

Sowing is an illustration of goodness, righteousness and fruit of attitude and good character. Seeds of what? Fruits of the spirit. For Galatians 5: 22-23 (AMP) says, "**But the fruit of the [Holy] Spirit [the work which His presence within accomplishes] is love, joy (gladness), peace, patience (an even temper, forbearance), kindness, goodness (benevolence), faithfulness,**

23 Gentleness (meekness, humility), self-control (self-restraint, continence). Against such things there is no law [[a]that can bring a charge]."

Then in Ephesians 1: 2-14 (AMP) it says, **"May grace (God's unmerited favor) and spiritual peace [which means peace with God and harmony, unity, and undisturbedness] be yours from God our Father and from the Lord Jesus Christ.**

3 May blessing (praise, laudation, and eulogy) be to the God and Father of our Lord Jesus Christ (the Messiah) Who has blessed us *in Christ* with every spiritual (given by the Holy Spirit) blessing in the heavenly realm!

4 Even as [in His love] He chose us [actually picked us out for Himself as His own] in Christ before the foundation of the world, that we should be holy (consecrated and set apart for Him) and blameless in His sight, *even* above reproach, before Him in love.

⁵ For He foreordained us (destined us, planned in love for us) to be adopted (revealed) as His own children through Jesus Christ, in accordance with the purpose of His will [[a]because it pleased Him and was His kind intent]—

⁶ [So that we might be] to the praise *and* the commendation of His glorious grace (favor and mercy), which He so freely bestowed on us in the Beloved.

⁷ In Him we have redemption (deliverance and salvation) through His blood, the remission (forgiveness) of our offenses (shortcomings and trespasses), in accordance with the riches *and* the generosity of His gracious favor,

⁸ Which He lavished upon us in every kind of wisdom and understanding (practical insight and prudence),

⁹ Making known to us the mystery (secret) of His will (of His plan, of His purpose). [And it is this:] In accordance with His good pleasure (His merciful intention) which He had previously purposed *and* set forth in [b]Him,

¹⁰ [He planned] for the maturity of the times *and* the climax of the ages to unify all things *and* head them up *and* consummate them in Christ, [both] things in heaven and things on the earth.

¹¹ In Him we also were made [God's] heritage (portion) *and* we obtained an inheritance; for we had been foreordained (chosen and appointed beforehand) in accordance with His purpose, Who works out everything in agreement with the counsel *and* design of His [own] will,

12 So that we who first hoped in Christ [who first put our confidence in Him have been destined and appointed to] live for the praise of His glory!

13 In Him you also who have heard the Word of Truth, the glad tidings (Gospel) of your salvation, and have believed in *and* adhered to *and* relied on Him, were stamped with the seal of the long-promised Holy Spirit.

14 That [Spirit] is the guarantee of our inheritance [the firstfruits, the pledge and foretaste, the down payment on our heritage], in anticipation of its full redemption *and* our acquiring [complete] possession of it—to the praise of His glory.

It has stated clearly that the Holy Spirit is our down payment of inheritance and Yahweh's kindness intent in love, through also the shedding of his blood and salvation we receive freely!

Hocus pocus verbal acts telling or asking you to sow your seed of money and tithing because the anointing is here you're going to miss it is Witchcraft! To receive his favor is free, also of course through the acts of obedience. We will get to the word sow or sowing some more.

Ephesians 2: 11-22 (AMP) says, **"Therefore, remember that at one time you were Gentiles (heathens) in the flesh, called Uncircumcision by those who called themselves Circumcision, [itself a [a]mere mark] in the flesh made by human hands.**

12 [Remember] that you were at that time separated (living apart) from Christ [excluded from all part in Him],

utterly estranged *and* outlawed from the rights of Israel as a nation, and strangers with no share in the sacred compacts of the [Messianic] promise [with no knowledge of or right in God's agreements, His covenants]. And you had no hope (no promise); you were in the world without God.

[13] But now in Christ Jesus, you who once were [so] far away, through (by, in) the blood of Christ have been brought near.

[14] For He is [Himself] our peace (our bond of unity and harmony). He has made us both [Jew and Gentile] one [body], and has broken down (destroyed, abolished) the hostile dividing wall between us,

[15] By abolishing in His [own crucified] flesh the enmity [caused by] the Law with its decrees and ordinances [which He annulled]; that He from the two might create in Himself one new man [one new quality of humanity out of the two], so making peace.

[16] And [He designed] to reconcile to God both [Jew and Gentile, united] in a single body by means of His cross, thereby killing the mutual enmity *and* bringing the feud to an end.

[17] And He came and preached the glad tidings of peace to you who were afar off and [peace] to those who were near.

[18] For it is through Him that we both [whether far off or near] now have an introduction (access) by one [Holy]

Spirit to the Father [so that we are able to approach Him].

¹⁹ Therefore you are no longer outsiders (exiles, migrants, and aliens, excluded from the rights of citizens), but you now share citizenship with the saints (God's own people, consecrated and set apart for Himself); and you belong to God's [own] household.

²⁰ You are built upon the foundation of the apostles and prophets with Christ Jesus Himself the chief Cornerstone.

²¹ In Him the whole structure is joined (bound, welded) together harmoniously, and it continues to rise (grow, increase) into a holy temple in the Lord [a sanctuary dedicated, consecrated, and sacred to the presence of the Lord].

²² In Him [and in fellowship with one another] you yourselves also are being built up [into this structure] with the rest, to form a fixed abode (dwelling place) of God in (by, through) the Spirit.

Anthony Montoya

Chapter Four

Tithing

Tithing was covenant in the Old Testament, notice verse 14-15, he came to make the two groups one and has destroyed the barrier, the dividing wall of hostility, by setting aside in his flesh the (The Law with its commands and regulations). Ponder on this for a few seconds let read Hebrews 7:5 (AMP), **"And it is true that those descendants of Levi who are charged with the priestly office are commanded in the Law to take tithes from the people—which means, from their brethren—though these have descended from Abraham.**

It was a law to take tithes from the children of Israel, so let's now move on to verse 12, **"For when there is a change in the priesthood, there is of necessity an alteration of the law [concerning the priesthood] as well.**

It specifically states the law changes oh my, last conclusion in verse 18, **"So a previous physical regulation *and* command is cancelled because of its weakness *and* ineffectiveness and uselessness—** Wow did you read that from the bible the regulation and command from verse five tithing is canceled word for word.

Most of us Christians have been demonically confused and driven to sow seeds of money and tithe manipulating us to receive God's unmerited favor and grace, making you feel abandoned, rejected and guilty. Apparently most of the time, Christians need healing and deliverance like never before your driven because of your own insecurity issues, you want to feel welcomed, accepted, desperately searching for attention, cared for feel loved and trusted that your somebody and have something to offer or be a part of and will do anything to attain it of course, it's understandable. Yearning to feel appreciated, let's read in the book of Peter.

2 Peter 2: 13-19 (AMP) says, **"Being destined to receive [punishment as] the reward of [their] unrighteousness [suffering wrong as the hire for their wrongdoing]. They count it a delight to revel in the daytime [living luxuriously and delicately]. They are blots and blemishes, reveling in their [a]deceptions** *and* **carousing together [even] as they feast with you.**

14 They have eyes full of harlotry, insatiable for sin. They beguile *and* **bait** *and* **lure away unstable souls. Their hearts are trained in covetousness (lust, greed), [they are] children of a curse [[b]exposed to cursing]!**

15 Forsaking the straight road they have gone astray; they have followed the way of Balaam [the son] of Beor, who loved the reward of wickedness.

16 But he was rebuked for his own transgression when a dumb beast of burden spoke with human voice and checked the prophet's madness.

17 These are springs without water and mists driven along before a tempest, for whom is reserved *forever* **the gloom of darkness. 18 For uttering loud boasts of folly, they beguile** *and* **lure with lustful desires of the flesh those who are barely escaping from them who are wrongdoers.**

¹⁹ They promise them liberty, when they themselves are the slaves of depravity *and* defilement—for by whatever anyone is made inferior *or* worse *or* is overcome, to that [person or thing] he is enslaved.

Saints, did your read verse 13, for they preach let's not forsake the fellowship of the saints, their motive and intentions operating in different spirits, Camellia spirits, transforming colors, slizzering, using web like filters in the spirit also shooting webs attaching them to your souls, a cockatrice spirit body of a snake head of a rooster, the head of rooster speaks like an a bold like manner in authority figure protecting the other chicken or ordering them like a task master.

Spiritual cloning devices, usually you are confused and misled because you're so gullible. Webster's online dictionary says (A cockatrice is a mythical beast, essentially a two-legged dragon with a rooster's head).

Anthony Montoya

Chapter 5

The Parable Of The Sower

In Matthew 13: 1-23 (AMP) we read, "**That same day Jesus went out of the house and was sitting beside the sea.**

² **But such great crowds gathered about Him that He got into a boat and remained sitting there, while all the throng stood on the shore.**

³ **And He told them many things in parables (stories by way of illustration and comparison), saying, A sower went out to sow.**

⁴ **And as he sowed, some seeds fell by the roadside, and the birds came and ate them up.**

⁵ **Other seeds fell on rocky ground, where they had not much soil; and at once they sprang up, because they had no depth of soil.**

⁶ **But when the sun rose, they were scorched, and because they had no root, they dried up *and* withered away.**

⁷ **Other seeds fell among thorns, and the thorns grew up and choked them out.** ⁸ **Other seeds fell on good soil, and yielded grain—some a hundred times as much as was sown, some sixty times as much, and some thirty.**

⁹ He who has ears [to hear], let him be listening *and* let him [a]consider *and* [b]perceive *and* comprehend by hearing.

¹⁰ Then the disciples came to Him and said, Why do You speak to them in parables?

¹¹ And He replied to them, To you it has been given to know the secrets *and* mysteries of the kingdom of heaven, but to them it has not been given.

¹² For whoever has [spiritual knowledge], to him will more be given *and* he will [c]be furnished richly so that he will have abundance; but from him who has not, even what he has will be taken away.

¹³ This is the reason that I speak to them in parables: because [d]having the power of seeing, they do not see; and [e]having the power of hearing, they do not hear, nor do they grasp *and* understand.

¹⁴ In them indeed is [f]the process of fulfillment of the prophecy of Isaiah, which says: You shall indeed hear *and* hear but never grasp *and* understand; and you shall indeed look *and* look but never see *and* perceive.

¹⁵ For this nation's heart has grown gross (fat and dull), and their ears heavy *and* difficult of hearing, and their eyes they have tightly closed, lest they see *and* perceive with their eyes, and hear *and* comprehend the sense with their ears, and grasp *and* understand with their heart, and turn *and* I should heal them.

¹⁶ But blessed (happy, fortunate, and [g]to be envied) are your eyes because they do see, and your ears because they do hear.

¹⁷ Truly I tell you, many prophets and righteous men [men who were upright and in right standing with God] yearned to see what you see, and did not see it, and to hear what you hear, and did not hear it.

¹⁸ Listen then to the [meaning of the] parable of the sower:

¹⁹ [h]While anyone is hearing the Word of the kingdom and does not grasp *and* comprehend it, the evil one comes and snatches away what was sown in his heart. This is what was sown along the roadside.

²⁰ As for what was sown on thin (rocky) soil, this is he who hears the Word and at once welcomes *and* accepts it with joy;

²¹ Yet it has no real root in him, but is temporary (inconstant, [i]lasts but a little while); and when affliction *or* trouble *or* persecution comes on account of the Word, at once he is caused to stumble [he is repelled and [i]begins to distrust and desert Him Whom he ought to trust and obey] *and* he falls away.

²² As for what was sown among thorns, this is he who hears the Word, but the cares of the world and the pleasure *and* delight *and* glamour *and* deceitfulness of riches choke *and* suffocate the Word, and it yields no fruit.

²³ As for what was sown on good soil, this is he who hears the Word and grasps *and* comprehends it; he indeed bears fruit and yields in one case a hundred times as much as was sown, in another sixty times as much, and in another thirty.

Wow, the reverse parapsychology when a preacher states sow your seed of money and may it increase 30, 60 and 100 fold blessing, what such hocus pocus. Sowing refers to the Word of God and how much its being implanted within you and the message not money. How much are you being planted in his word?

Let's now refer to 2 Corinthians 9: 6-12 (AMP) which reads, **"[Remember] this: he who sows sparingly *and* grudgingly will also reap sparingly *and* grudgingly, and he who sows generously [[a]that blessings may come to someone] will also reap generously *and* with blessings.**

⁷ Let each one [give] as he has made up his own mind *and* purposed in his heart, not reluctantly *or* sorrowfully or under compulsion, for God loves (He [b]takes pleasure in, prizes above other things, and is unwilling to abandon or to do without) a cheerful (joyous, "prompt to do it") giver [whose heart is in his giving].

⁸ And God is able to make all grace (every favor and [c]earthly blessing) come to you in abundance, so that you may always *and* under all circumstances *and* whatever the need [d]be self-sufficient [possessing enough to require no aid or support and furnished in abundance for every good work and charitable donation].

⁹ As it is written, He [the benevolent person] scatters abroad; He gives to the poor; His deeds of justice *and* goodness *and* kindness *and* benevolence will go on *and* endure forever!

¹⁰ And [God] Who provides seed for the sower and bread for eating will also provide and multiply your [resources for] sowing and increase the fruits of your righteousness [[e]which manifests itself in active goodness, kindness, and charity].

¹¹ Thus you will be enriched in all things *and* in every way, so that you can be generous, and [your generosity as it is] administered by us will bring forth thanksgiving to God.

¹² For the service that the ministering of this fund renders does not only fully supply what is lacking to the saints (God's people), but it also overflows in many [cries of] thanksgiving to God."

The heavenly Father speaks of sowing as the attitude of the Heart not money. What are you reaping of the message and how much there are levels of long suffering, kindness, forgiveness, correct? When you sow a seed in plantation, what needs to happen is it needs to fall into the ground and break and die first saints, then what kind of fruits of righteousness does it produce and how much?

Matthew 21: 44 says, **"And whosoever shall fall on this stone shall be broken; but on whomsoever it shall fall, it will grind him to powder."**

Unless a seed falls to the ground it cannot produce, this is not an illustration of money saints, sowing the father speaks of this laying your life down at the altar of Yashua's feet meaning consecrate yourselves to meet with the Father face to face. They speak of sow your seed of money by faith, for by faith you cannot please God.

Galatians 5:6 (AMP) says, **"For [if we are] in Christ Jesus, neither circumcision nor uncircumcision counts for anything, but only faith activated *and* energized *and* expressed *and* working through love."**

Here again in the word of Yahweh, faith is worked by love, what are your motives and intentions For [if we are] in Christ Jesus, neither circumcision nor uncircumcision counts for anything, but only faith activated *and* energized *and* expressed *and* working through love. For [if we are] in Christ Jesus, neither circumcision nor uncircumcision counts for anything, but only faith activated *and* energized *and* expressed *and* working through love of the heart. Yes I truly believe in giving in honor of course, give to what you have purposed in your heart not the witchcraft sow into God's kingdom with your money and tithing. The spirit and revelation of provision is a pure heart, obedience and lead by the Holy Spirit of his instructions.

Let's read the book of Jude, which says, **"Jude, a servant of Jesus Christ (the Messiah), and brother of James, [writes this letter] to those who are called (chosen), dearly loved by God the Father *and separated (set apart)* and kept for Jesus Christ:**

[2] May mercy, [soul] peace, and love be multiplied to you.

[3] Beloved, my whole concern was to write to you in regard to our common salvation. [But] I found it necessary *and* was impelled to write you and urgently appeal to *and* exhort [you] to contend for the faith which was once for all [a]handed down to the saints [the faith

which is that sum of Christian belief which was delivered [b]verbally to the holy people of God].

⁴For certain men have crept in stealthily [[c]gaining entrance secretly by a side door]. Their doom was predicted long ago, ungodly (impious, profane) persons who pervert the grace (the spiritual blessing and favor) of our God into lawlessness *and* wantonness *and* immorality, and disown *and* deny our sole Master and Lord, Jesus Christ (the Messiah, the Anointed One).

⁵Now I want to remind you, though you were fully informed once for all, that though the Lord [at one time] delivered a people out of the land of Egypt, He subsequently destroyed those [of them] who did not believe [who refused to adhere to, trust in, and rely upon Him].

⁶And angels who did not keep (care for, guard, and hold to) their own first place of power but abandoned their proper dwelling place—these He has reserved in custody in eternal chains (bonds) under the thick gloom of utter darkness until the judgment *and* doom of the great day.

⁷[The wicked are sentenced to suffer] just as Sodom and Gomorrah and the adjacent towns—which likewise gave themselves over to impurity and indulged in unnatural vice *and* sensual perversity—are laid out [in plain sight] as an exhibit of perpetual punishment [to warn] of everlasting fire.

⁸Nevertheless in like manner, these dreamers also corrupt the body, scorn *and* reject authority *and*

government, and revile *and* libel *and* scoff at [heavenly] glories (the glorious ones).

⁹ But when [even] the archangel Michael, contending with the devil, judicially argued (disputed) about the body of Moses, he dared not [presume to] bring an abusive condemnation against him, but [simply] said, The Lord rebuke you!

¹⁰ But these men revile (scoff and sneer at) anything they do not happen to be acquainted with *and* do not understand; and whatever they do understand physically [that which they know by mere instinct], like irrational beasts—by these they corrupt themselves *and* are destroyed (perish).

¹¹ Woe to them! For they have run riotously in the way of Cain, and have abandoned themselves for the sake of gain [it offers them, following] the error of Balaam, and have perished in rebellion [like that] of Korah!

¹² These are hidden reefs (elements of danger) in your love feasts, where they boldly feast sumptuously [carousing together in your midst], without scruples providing for themselves [alone]. They are clouds without water, swept along by the winds; trees, without fruit at the late autumn gathering time—twice (doubly) dead, [lifeless and] plucked up by the roots;

¹³ Wild waves of the sea, flinging up the foam of their own shame *and* disgrace; wandering stars, for whom the gloom of eternal darkness has been reserved forever.

14 It was of these people, moreover, that Enoch in the seventh [generation] from Adam prophesied when he said, Behold, the Lord comes with His myriads of holy ones (ten thousands of His saints)

15 To execute judgment upon all and to convict all the impious (unholy ones) of all their ungodly deeds which they have committed [in such an] ungodly [way], and of all the severe (abusive, jarring) things which ungodly sinners have spoken against Him.

16 These are inveterate murmurers (grumblers) who complain [of their lot in life], going after their own desires [controlled by their passions]; their talk is boastful *and* arrogant, [and they claim to] admire men's persons *and* pay people flattering compliments to gain advantage.

17 But you must remember, beloved, the predictions which were made by the apostles (the special messengers) of our Lord Jesus Christ (the Messiah, the Anointed One).

18 They told you beforehand, In the last days (in the end time) there will be scoffers [who seek to gratify their own unholy desires], following after their own ungodly passions.

19 It is these who are [agitators] setting up distinctions *and* causing divisions—merely sensual [creatures, carnal, worldly-minded people], devoid of the [Holy] Spirit *and* destitute of any higher spiritual life.

^{20} But you, beloved, build yourselves up [founded] on your most holy faith [[d]make progress, rise like an edifice higher and higher], praying in the Holy Spirit;

^{21} Guard *and* keep yourselves in the love of God; expect *and* patiently wait for the mercy of our Lord Jesus Christ (the Messiah)—[which will bring you] unto life eternal.

^{22} And *refute [so as to] convict some who dispute with you, and* on some have mercy who waver *and* doubt.

^{23} [Strive to] save others, snatching [them] out of [the] fire; on others take pity [but] with fear, loathing even the garment spotted by the flesh *and* polluted by their sensuality.

^{24} Now to Him Who is able to keep you without stumbling *or* slipping *or* falling, and to present [you] unblemished (blameless and faultless) before the presence of His glory in triumphant joy *and* exultation [with unspeakable, ecstatic delight]—

^{25} To the one only God, our Savior through Jesus Christ our Lord, be glory (splendor), majesty, might *and* dominion, and power *and* authority, before all time and now and forever (unto all the ages of eternity). Amen (so be it).

Chapter 6

Different Winds Of Doctrine

Let's clarify some more conditions you might have questions about also. Seed is what we were speaking of, what kind of seeds need to die. Remember illustrating seed need to go down and crack and then die and then resurrect to what kind of fruit is produced in your hearts of righteousness not darkness. You cannot mix The Old Covenant and The New Covenant.

Ephesians 1:14 (AMP) says, **"That [Spirit] is the guarantee of our inheritance [the firstfruits, the pledge and foretaste, the down payment on our heritage], in anticipation of its full redemption** *and* **our acquiring [complete] possession of it—to the praise of His glory."**

Christians have received seeds of misconceptions about honoring Hashem with your tithe that's Old Covenant. Really, let's look at Hebrews 8:13 (AMP) which says, **"When God speaks of a new [covenant or agreement], He makes the first one obsolete (out of use). And what is obsolete (out of use and annulled because of age) is ripe for disappearance** *and* **to be dispensed with altogether."**

Tithing was covenant hello, it does not state in the word that sowing seed money to break a curse, so what you're really illustrating is that you're sowing, tithing and your human regulations and commands are more important than Yahshua's blood and the Holy Spirit. Alright let me clarify this injunction, if the tithe and sowing your seed of money rebukes the devour and the locusts from eating your crops of increase, why would there be a need to have your Pastor, Prophet, Apostle etc. to pray for you or prophecy favor, prosperity and finances over you if the tithing does it.

Show me in the book of the Holy Bible where Yahshua or the Apostles after moving in the gifts of the spirit with demonstration and power, deliverance and healing asked them to sow of seed of money before you go from me. Yes, the Father honors when you sow into the kingdom with money of course he loves you when it's your heart in it.

What I'm saying is don't be misled or directed by the different winds of doctrines, which is false impregnation, false hope and hope differed makes the heart sick and weary. Here is the real recollection of it all. Most christians want the lazy way out, thinking if I sow money or tithe increase in all directions come, meaning you're too lazy or stubborn or rebellious or disobedient to let go or stop what you have been instructed to do. Meaning what stop eating sugar. God told you to stay away from ungodly family or Christian soul ties, he is asking of your time alone with him, he told you to have boundaries and accept responsibility, he told you to pray more or worship me more. He told you to do something he told you to let go of bitterness, unforgiveness, jealousy, envy, pride etc. Many of us have accepted our profits of gain, complacency, compromise and self-denial, but remember it states in the word some will barely escape!

2 Corinthians 8: 8-13 (AMP) says, **"I give this not as an order [to dictate to you], but to prove, by [pointing out] the zeal of others, the sincerity of your [own] love also.**

⁹ For you are becoming progressively acquainted with *and* recognizing more strongly *and* clearly the grace of our Lord Jesus Christ (His kindness, His gracious generosity, His undeserved favor and spiritual blessing), [in] that though He was [so very] rich, yet for your sakes He became [so very] poor, in order that by His poverty you might become enriched (abundantly supplied).

¹⁰ [It is then] my counsel *and* my opinion in this matter that I give [you when I say]: It is profitable *and* fitting for you [now to complete the enterprise] which more than a year ago you not only began, but were the first to wish to do anything [about contributions for the relief of the saints at Jerusalem].

¹¹ So now finish doing it, that your [enthusiastic] readiness in desiring it may be equalled by your completion of it according to your ability *and* means.

¹² For if the [eager] readiness to give is there, then it is acceptable *and* welcomed in proportion to what a person has, not according to what he does not have.

¹³ For it is not [intended] that other people be eased *and* relieved [of their responsibility] and you be burdened *and* suffer [unfairly]"

In Luke 18: 9-14 (AMP), Jesus tells a parable of a Pharisee and a tax collector who go the the temple to pray. The Pharisee boasts of his tithing, among other things and the tax collector simply asks for mercy (nothing is mentioned of tithing in the case of the tax collector). Yet in this parable, the tax collector, not the Pharisee, goes away justified (of course, the primary focus of this parable, as of being justified without tithing, or not being justified despite tithing, is still present).

Continue in point, references in scripture, 1 Corinthians 9: 3-10, "What is my reward then? Verily that, when I preach the gospel, I may make the good news of Yahshua without charge".... One of the Apostles asked a question according to his life living as a sacrificial blessing for others.

Let's read 2 Corinthians 6: 3-11 (AMP), **"We put no obstruction in anybody's way [we give no offense in anything], so that no fault may be found *and* [our] ministry blamed *and* discredited.**

4 But we commend ourselves in every way as [true] servants of God: through great endurance, in tribulation *and* suffering, in hardships *and* privations, in sore straits *and* calamities,

5 In beatings, imprisonments, riots, labors, sleepless watching, hunger;

6 By innocence *and* purity, knowledge *and* spiritual insight, longsuffering *and* patience, kindness, in the Holy Spirit, in unfeigned love;

7 By [speaking] the word of truth, in the power of God, with the weapons of righteousness for the right hand [to attack] and for the left hand [to defend];

8 Amid honor and dishonor; in defaming *and* evil report and in praise *and* good report. [We are branded] as deceivers (impostors), and [yet vindicated as] truthful *and* honest.

⁹ [We are treated] as unknown *and* ignored [by the world], and [yet we are] well-known *and* recognized [by God and His people]; as dying, and yet here we are alive; as chastened by suffering and [yet] not killed;

¹⁰ As grieved *and* mourning, yet [we are] always rejoicing; as poor [ourselves, yet] bestowing riches on many; as having nothing, and [yet in reality] possessing all things.

¹¹ Our mouth is open to you, Corinthians [we are hiding nothing, keeping nothing back], and our heart is expanded wide [for you]!"

Notice Paul's heart and experience for the sake of Yahshua to live as a life giving sacrifice for others and gratitude and contentent. Don't be manipulated when someone is asking for money with flattery, telling you it's better to give than to receive, this quotation from the word has been sourly misused. As a minister of the good news we live as a sacrifical blessing for others, it says signs and wonders shall follow thee meaning, provision will always be supplied to the one who looses his life for the kingdom!

Matthew 19: 29 says, **"And everyone that has forsaken houses, or brothers, or sisters, or father, or mother, or wife or children or lands for my name's sake shall receive a hundredfold and shall inherit everlasting life."**

Let's review Malachi in detail about tithing. Malachi 1: 6-14 (AMP) which says, **"A son honors his father, and a servant his master. If then I am a Father, where is My honor? And if I am a Master, where is the [reverent] fear due Me? says the Lord of hosts to you, O priests, who** despise My name. You say, How *and* in what way have we despised Your name?

⁷ By offering polluted food upon My altar. And you ask, How have we polluted it *and* profaned You? By thinking that the table of the Lord is contemptible *and* may be despised.

⁸ When you [priests] offer blind [animals] for sacrifice, is it not evil? And when you offer the lame and the sick, is it not evil? Present such a thing [a blind or lame or sick animal] now to your governor [in payment of your taxes, and see what will happen]. Will he be pleased with you? Or will he receive you graciously? says the Lord of hosts.

⁹ Now then, I [Malachi] beg [you priests], entreat God [earnestly] that He will be gracious to us. With such a gift from your hand [as a defective animal for sacrifice], will He accept it *or* show favor to any of you? says the Lord of hosts.

¹⁰ Oh, that there were even one among you [whose duty it is to minister to Me] who would shut the doors, that you might not kindle fire on My altar to no purpose [an empty, futile, fruitless pretense]! I have no pleasure in you, says the Lord of hosts, nor will I accept an offering from your hand.

¹¹ For from the rising of the sun to its setting My name shall be great among the nations, and in every place incense shall be offered to My name, and indeed a pure offering; for My name shall be great among the nations, says the Lord of hosts.

¹² But you [priests] profane it when [by your actions] you say, The table of the Lord is polluted, and the fruit of it, its food, is contemptible *and* may be despised.

¹³ You say also, Behold, what a drudgery *and* weariness this is! And you have sniffed at it, says the Lord of hosts. And you have brought that which was [a]taken by violence, or the lame or the sick; this you bring as an offering! Shall I accept this from your hand? says the Lord.

¹⁴ But cursed is the [cheating] deceiver who has a male in his flock and vows to offer it, yet sacrifices to the [sovereign] Lord a blemished *or* diseased thing! For I am a great King, says the Lord of hosts, and My name is terrible *and* to be [reverently] feared among the nations." This whole chapter is talking to the priests family.

Malachi 2: 1-8 (AMP) says, "And now, O you priests, this commandment is for you.

² If you will not hear and if you will not lay it to heart to give glory to My name, says the Lord of hosts, then I will send the curse upon you, and I will curse your blessings; yes, I have already turned them to curses because you do not lay it to heart.

³ Behold, I will rebuke your seed [grain—which will prevent due harvest], and I will spread the [a]dung from the festival offerings upon your faces, and you shall be taken away with it.

⁴ And you shall know, recognize, *and* understand that I have sent this [new] decree to you priests, to be My [new] covenant with Levi [the priestly tribe], says the Lord of hosts.

⁵ My covenant [on My part with Levi] was to give him life and peace, because [on his part] of the [reverent and worshipful] fear with which [the priests] would revere Me and stand in awe of My name.

⁶ The law of truth was in [Levi's] mouth, and unrighteousness was not found in his lips; he walked with Me in peace and uprightness and turned many away from iniquity.

⁷ For the priest's lips should guard *and* keep pure the knowledge [of My law], and the people should seek (inquire for and require) instruction at his mouth; for he is the messenger of the Lord of hosts.

⁸ But you have turned aside out of the way; you have caused many to stumble by your instruction [in the law]; you have corrupted the covenant of Levi [with Me], says the Lord of hosts." The heavenly Father is still speaking about the priest! The Levites.

Malachi 3:3 (AMP) says, **"He will sit as a refiner and purifier of silver, and He will purify the priests, the sons of Levi, and refine them like gold and silver, that they may offer to the Lord offerings in righteousness."** The Father is stil speaking about the robbers, the priests, about refining them!

Revelation explains verse 8-11 (AMP), **"Will a man rob or defraud God?** Yet you rob and defraud Me. But you say, in what way do we rob or defraud you? (You have withheld your) tithes and offerings."

⁹ You are cursed with the curse, for you are robbing Me, even this whole nation.

¹⁰ Bring all the tithes (the whole tenth of your income) into the storehouse, that there may be food in My house, and prove Me now by it, says the Lord of hosts, if I will not open the windows of heaven for you and pour you out a blessing, that there shall not be room enough to receive it.

¹¹ And I will rebuke the devourer [insects and plagues] for your sakes and he shall not destroy the fruits of your ground, neither shall your vine drop its fruit before the time in the field, says the Lord of hosts.

Prophetically speaking about the tithe, first of all most of the Israelites were farmers in agriculture. Bring the tithes into the storehouse, that there may be meat in my house! The tithe means one one tenth of a whole, God wants our complete reverence, wholehartedly, storehouse (We are the temple of the Holy Spirit), so your wondering of what does "meat" mean?

Paul the Apostle in the New Covenant speaks of "meat." 1 Corinthians 3:1-3, which says, **"However, brethren, I could not talk to you as to spiritual [men], but as to nonspiritual [men of the flesh, in whom the carnal nature predominates], as to mere infants [in the new life] in Christ [[a]unable to talk yet!]**

² I fed you with milk, not solid food, for you were not yet strong enough [to be ready for it]; but even yet you are not strong enough [to be ready for it],

³ For you are still [unspiritual, having the nature] of the flesh [under the control of ordinary impulses]. For as long as [there are] envying and jealousy *and* wrangling and factions among you, are you not unspiritual *and* of the flesh, behaving yourselves after a human standard *and* like mere (unchanged) men?"

God speaks of immaturity and maturity of the meat of his word and the fruits of the spirit of a transformed circumsized hert. Now when the word applies to the Old Covenant talking to Israel only, they were farmer's family and he said he would prevent pests and plagues from devouring their crops. If you're not a farmer or have no clue what a farmer does, then you would not understand about the different ailments according to farming that can harm crops. When the Father spoke of the Blessing pouring out, what did the farmers need to tithe their portions family.

The farmers neeed rain water for crops to produce, if it did not rain how were the children of Israel were allowed to tithe to the Levites, the Levites would have nothing if it didn't rain for several months or years.

The time of blessing is over, blessings pertain to (Portion or Portions when it comes or doesn't you have to wait cause of drought or hold up).

Chapter 7

Our Inheritance

Today in 2014, there has been an alert on water shortage in different cities in California. Some cities were fined a numerous amount of money for washing their cars after a certain time or sprinklers on too long, because it hadn't rained much. The alert went to Level 4, no water, even the prices of food distribution has gone up sky high.

So what is at hand here? You read in the beginning of this book about God's favor and increase and Our Holy Spirit is the guarantee to our inheritance, always available in obedience, instructions and spiritual timing.

We are entering into the Promised Land, his fulfillment of scriptures, only to the remnant who has died to self and has endured trials and tribulations, those who have received a transformed circumcised heart. Even to those who are willing, but in everything that everyone believes in he honors and everyone has a personal relationship with God.

Micah 3: 11-12 (AMP) says, **"Its heads judge for reward *and* a bribe and its priests teach for hire and its prophets divine for money; yet they lean on the Lord and say, Is not the Lord among us? No evil can come upon us.**

12 Therefore shall Zion on your account be [a]plowed like a field, Jerusalem shall become heaps [of ruins], and the

mountain of the house [of the Lord] like a densely wooded height."

Then 2 Chronicles 31: 5-6 (AMP) says, **"As soon as the command went abroad, the Israelites gave in abundance the firstfruits of grain, vintage fruit, oil, honey, and of all the produce of the field; and they brought in abundantly the tithe of everything.**

⁶ **The people of Israel and Judah who lived in Judah's cities also brought the tithe of cattle and sheep and of the dedicated things which were consecrated to the Lord their God, and they laid them in heaps.**

Then in Nehemiah 13:5 (AMP) it says that they, **"Prepared for Tobiah a large chamber where previously they had put the cereal offerings, the frankincense, the vessels, and the tithes of grain, new wine, and oil which were given by commandment to the Levites, the singers, and gatekeepers, and the contributions for the priests.**

No where in the bible was the tithe given as money by people and families. Deuteronomy 14:29 (AMP) says, **"And the Levite [because he has no part or inheritance with you] and the stranger** *or* **temporary resident, and the fatherless and the widow who are in your towns shall come and eat and be satisfied, so that the Lord your God may bless you in all the work of your hands that you do."**

The strangers, fatherless and widows were to share in the blessings of the tithe for free, they didn't have to tithe at all.

My final conclusion will come from Deuteronomy 15: 5-10 (AMP) which says, **"If only you carefully listen to the voice of the Lord your God, to do watchfully all these commandments which I command you this day.**

⁶ When the Lord your God blesses you as He promised you, then you shall lend to many nations, but you shall not borrow; and you shall rule over many nations, but they shall not rule over you.

⁷ If there is among you a poor man, one of your kinsmen in any of the towns of your land which the Lord your God gives you, you shall not harden your [minds and] hearts or close your hands to your poor brother;

⁸ But you shall open your hands wide to him and shall surely lend him sufficient for his need in whatever he lacks.

⁹ Beware lest there be a base thought in your [minds and] hearts, and you say, The seventh year, the year of release, is at hand, and your eye be evil against your poor brother and you give him nothing, and he cry to the Lord against you, and it be sin in you.

¹⁰ You shall give to him freely without begrudging it; because of this the Lord will bless you in all your work and in all you undertake."

Wow, has anyone ever read or heard this scripture in TV land or congregational church buildings or conferences? It says, poor brother within thy gates, church, congregation, ministry, conferences and those involved in your circle in need.

What of any of these places give or pass out money from the tithe? It's okay, you all can laugh. It also states speaking to whoever is convinced or convicted, disturbed etc. When you give the portion what you give him should not grieve his heart, meaning just because you give him to what you think is righteous is not the affirming, the receiver that is in need his heart should be well pleased without any shadow of doubt!

One of the verses say, "If he cries because nothing was given to him he cries unto the Lord against thee and it be a sin unto thee." there must be a lot of sin going on in the church buildings. I haven't been to one church that passes out money since the tithe is all money! That means give me money all the time every church service.

Okay, you're probably using your carnal mentality of what justification you can come up with using analytical revenues or for a rebuttal of comprehension instead of being Christ like.

Yahshua's words in Matthew 5:42 (AMP) says, **"Give to him who keeps on begging from you, and do not turn away from him who would borrow [[a]at interest] from you."**

Ministry Contact Information

You may contact Anthony Montoya through the following sources:

Email Address:

Judah1231@yahoo.com

Website:

anthonymontoyas1.weebly.com

www.ingramcontent.com/pod-product-compliance
Lightning Source LLC
Chambersburg PA
CBHW060858050426
42453CB00008B/1010